The Essential Guide to Creative Entrepreneurship

Printed in the USA

First Edition

Title: The Essential Guide to Creative Entrepreneurship: Making and Selling Your Neon Yellow Tiger/David Andrew Wiebe, author.

ISBN: 9781793202369

Cover Design: Laganson Graphic Design

Interior Design and Layout: David Andrew Wiebe

Dedicated to The Indie YYC Community.

You inspire me to be better.

Contents

The Essential Guide to Creative Entrepreneurship

Making and Selling Your Neon Yellow Tiger

DAVID ANDREW WIEBE

Introduction

In the gig economy, side hustles have become increasingly popular.

For many, traditional job roles simply aren't cutting it. The Balance indicates that in October 2018, U.S. consumer debt rose 7.7% to $3.964 trillion. Credit card debt, auto loans and school loans account for most of this debt.

The Balance also points out that, while home mortgages are a major loan category, they don't classify it as debt–mortgages are considered a personal investment. I don't agree with that assessment, but that's beside the point.

Others pursue side hustles as a means of finding expression for their greatest passions. Whether it's to augment their income, spend time doing something that makes them come alive, or save up for a rainy day, there are plenty of good reasons to diversify and be less dependent on jobs to make a living.

Then, there are those whose side hustles have become their full-time hustle, in the form of a small, independent business. Whether it's selling hand-crafted jewelry on Etsy, publishing unique music videos to YouTube and monetizing them through Patreon, or taking on freelance graphic design work through a freelancing site like Upwork, there simply isn't a shortage of opportunities.

As someone who's been working entirely from home since summer 2016, I consider myself a proponent of the gig economy. Up until that point, I was dividing my time between ghostwriting and content work, audiovisual tech work at the University, helping organize and host unique creative events, teaching guitar and playing live gigs as a musician.

In case you're wondering whether I was "making it" during those years leading up to 2016, I was paying down my debt at a ferocious rate and even stockpiling my savings. But it was madness.

As my ghostwriting and content work started taking off, I decided to leave "organized chaos" behind so I could focus on what was becoming a more lucrative opportunity for me—ghostwriting and content work. That also freed me up to put more time and effort into creative communities, gigging and building my small, independent business—The Music Entrepreneur HQ.

As I look towards the future and what I'm planning to accomplish, I can see that the possibilities are nearly limitless. My small business doesn't need to stay small forever. My earning potential isn't capped. I can make my own hours and work when I'm at my personal best.

And, though outreach is still a crucial part of what I do, people often come to me wanting to work with me, whether it's independent musicians, music business owners or other creatives.

And, that's the same opportunity that's staring back at you.

This isn't to suggest that entrepreneurship–or freelancing, for that matter–is easy. But *it is* simple. It's all about finding a need and filling it. It's about serving a hungry audience and presenting a solution that's right for them.

But these ideas might seem a little elusive as a creative. You're bound to have many questions:

- How can I serve an audience with my art?
- Do I need to sell out to make it?
- Am I required to adapt my art so that it appeals to a larger audience?

And, the answer is "it depends". It depends on what you're hoping to achieve.

There's nothing wrong with creating art for the sake of creating art. If it fulfills you and you find joy in the process, I think that's worth more than any price tag you could put on it. And, if you're lucky, simply engaging in what you love can attract an audience.

As a musician, I've often created music that I wanted to create as opposed to music that fits a certain demographic's interests.

But I'm also under no delusion that this music will reach a huge audience and result in large sums of revenue. Music represents an important outlet for my creative self-expression, and to that end it will always serve my needs. Beyond that, it's anybody's guess.

But when it comes to serving my audience–namely creative entrepreneurs–that's a different matter entirely. I am focused on creating content that benefits them and helps them reach their goals, whatever they may be.

Adding value to others can take many forms. And, sometimes the things you put effort into don't always bear fruit. But I find the process fulfilling. Though I have certain business goals I want to reach, I'm more focused on the journey than on the destination. If I'm not enjoying the process, perhaps I'm not engaged in the right activity.

So, creative entrepreneurship may not be for everybody. But the good news is that you can pursue it at whatever level is right for you.

I know there are plenty of experts selling the idea of hustle out there. And, they talk endlessly about the fact that if you're not struggling, you're not getting anywhere. To succeed, you need to be pulling 14- to 16-hour days, butting your head against the wall, and if you're not, you're probably not going anywhere.

But I know for a fact that you don't need that type of work ethic to earn an extra $500 to $1,000 per month.

So, if that's your goal, you're probably not listening to the right people.

Go as far as you can, and then you'll see further. And, for you, going as far as you can might be starting a blog and sharing your poems on a weekly basis. There's nothing wrong with that. Maybe, in a few months, or in a few years, you'll want more. At that point, you can choose whether you're ready to commit to more.

The greater the desire, the more work you'll need to put in. But you don't need to start off with 16-hour work days, especially if your goals are humble.

In the chapters that follow, you will learn about various aspects of creative entrepreneurship, from marketing your art to building a team and a great deal more. The ideas and examples presented should help you navigate the road ahead, whatever that may look like.

This book is intended as an overview to creative entrepreneurship. But there are references to plenty of great tools and resources you can access throughout. If you need additional help, I suggest that you refer to these. And, if you have any questions, don't hesitate to reach out to me personally.

I wish you success on the journey ahead.

Tools & Resources

Consumer Debt Statistics: Definition, Causes, Impact – The Balance
https://www.thebalance.com/consumer-debt-statistics-causes-and-impact-3305704

Making Your Art

As a creative, you probably don't need to be told to work on your art. You would do it even if no one was paying you to do it. That's how much you love it. It's your passion.

I don't want to tell you how to do your creative work either. Whether it's taking photos, writing poetry or painting murals, you should be an expert at your craft already. If not, then keep going. Keep making more art. You will improve.

But there are a few things I want to share with you about the strategic aspect of making your art.

Serving an Audience

For many artists, their art serves them.

There's nothing wrong with this. If you love working on your art and it fulfills you, more power to you.

But if you consider yourself a creative entrepreneur, or you're thinking about becoming one, then you're going to want to take a different approach.

If your art only serves you, it can be an uphill slog trying to find an audience.

I once interviewed Jack Conte for my blog. He's one half of Pomplamoose and CEO of Patreon.

Pomplamoose found success on YouTube through the video song medium. But this didn't happen overnight.

Jack says they kept adapting and iterating until they found a formula that appealed to their audience. That involved taking popular songs, reharmonizing the chords, keeping the melody, adding unique instrumentation, and documenting it all in the form of a video song.

Some artists call this selling out. I just call it being mindful of what your audience wants.

If you want to find a market to sell your art to, make it your mission to serve an audience.

Being Prolific vs. Being a Perfectionist

People are now bombarded with texts, emails, instant messages, social media notifications and so on.

This underscores the importance of staying top of mind with your audience because they are being overwhelmed with information from every direction. And, if you want to stay top of mind, you're going to want to show up for them as often as possible.

Today, if you were to ask me whether it's better to be prolific or to be a perfectionist, I would tell you it's better to be *sustainably prolific*.

I admit that it's a loaded question. Some artists I know don't want to put out anything they can't ultimately be proud of.

I understand that perspective. The only problem is that a few years down the line, you may not feel the same way about it.

A "hit" can sometimes be a double-edged sword. Do you think Van Halen loved performing "Jump" every single time they went on tour? With all the touring they did, I imagine there were times when they didn't want to go on and play that song one more time.

So, what's perfect to you now may not be perfect to you a few years down the line. Do you see how that can be a trap?

If you want to keep your audience engaged, you need to keep sharing your art—even if it is half finished—preferably daily.

I'm not suggesting that it's a matter of quantity over quality. I'm suggesting that it's about finding a healthy balance between the two.

The reality is that your fans may end up liking the creations you hate, and you may end up liking the creations they hate. So, you can't make any assumptions about what people may take a liking to.

Hitting Two Birds with One Stone

Let's say you're an illustrator. You love to draw and create pictures.

But you're also tech savvy. You understand how search engine algorithms and keywords work.

So, you begin producing new drawings every single day, as often as you can. These works are then shared on your blog, Behance, Etsy, DeviantArt and other sites.

Now, you know how hard it can be to stand out as an illustrator. But because you're creating new work every single day and sharing it with the world, you're going to pick up momentum.

This is particularly true if you choose an underserved niche. You *could* spend your time drawing a lot of different things. But if you did that, it would take you a while to gain attention for your work.

Meanwhile, if you spent all your time drawing purple dragons, and you had hundreds of purple dragon drawings, you would dominate that niche. Trust me–I looked it up, and the competition isn't that stiff (as of this writing).

The added benefit being that if someone searched for a purple dragon in Google and clicked on "Images", they would see your work. So, not only would you be serving a niche audience, you would be effectively marketing your work as you're creating it. You would be hitting two birds with one stone.

In general, I don't find artists love marketing. So, if your creating and marketing efforts went hand in hand, it could make your life a lot easier.

This is the ideal to strive for, but it isn't possible in every situation. Sometimes you will have to prioritize your marketing efforts–publishing blog posts, sharing your work on social media, sending emails to your audience and more.

But can you see how being prolific would play right into hitting two birds with one stone?

Planning for Success

So, you need to make your art. But you also need to promote it. There's no two ways about this.

What many artists do is create their art and hope that someone will discover it and like it enough to give them the permission they need to succeed.

This is not the way the world works anymore. You need to be the first to make your presence known. You need to be able to communicate your value to others.

So, why not plan for success?

Create a strategy for yourself. Consider how you'll be marketing your art. Think about how much time you'll be spending on it. Research and find the best channels for sharing your work with the world.

Your plan doesn't need to be perfect. What matters is that you have a plan.

You can't steer a parked car. But once you get going, it becomes much easier to know when you need to course correct. Just ensure that you have a clear destination in mind. If you don't, you won't know when you are off track.

One thing my mentors taught me was that success doesn't happen by accident. It requires planning. So, be intentional about the steps you take to get to where you want to go.

Your Art is Your Business

Every business has a product or service to sell.

Your product is your art.

Set aside any preconceptions you may have about marketing and selling your art, such as how much you can charge for it or whether people will buy it.

If you make it and get it in front of people, you will discover that many people are willing to pay good money for your creations.

But you do need to find a way to get it in front of them first. That's key.

Tools & Resources

I Asked Jack Conte About Success... Here's What He Shared With Me
http://www.musicentrepreneurhq.com/conte

Targeting a Niche

Make no mistake about it–your art does *not* appeal to everyone.

And, there are no clear dividing lines between interests anymore. Some people who love the blues also love EDM. Some who love portraits also love landscapes. Others who enjoy abstract poetry might be into something mostly unrelated like macramé.

Further, we know that people don't just follow one person on social media. They follow a variety of people, even if it's in the same industry.

Understanding this behavior is key to targeting a niche. After all, you'll need to cut through the noise if you want to stand out.

Standing Out from the Crowd

Let's say you're a visual artist. Well, I can tell you right now that you're not the only visual artist out there. So, that alone will not make you stand out from the crowd.

What has the potential to help you cut through the noise is your subject matter (what you draw or paint), your style (the specific way in which you draw or paint), and the medium (the tools you use to draw or paint).

When I Google the term "tiger painting", it turns up 101 million search results. That number instantly goes down to 21.8 million results if I enter the term, "neon yellow tiger painting" instead. And, when I look at the image results, I don't see too many legitimate neon yellow tigers (though if you enter other common colors like blue or green, you will).

This example should go to illustrate that you probably have a better chance at being recognized for your neon yellow tiger paintings than your generic tiger paintings.

I'm not going to stop you from putting together a tiger painting if that's your heart's desire, but again, there are plenty of these out there. So, you're probably not going to find your audience this way.

From General to Specific

Targeting a niche is the last thing most creatives want to do. They don't like to be pigeonholed. Plus, they want to be free to create whatever they want to create.

Yet if I told you to sit down and write, draw, paint, or sculpt right now, without any further instructions, you might be at a loss as to what to create. And, even if you did make something, it might not be terribly inspired.

So, I think you would agree that determining a focus for your piece before getting to work on it is important.

What's the point? The point is that, as a creative entrepreneur, you should begin with at least a general sense of what genre of art you're going to be creating.

If you're a country artist, then write country songs. Writing a rock song might be fun, but if you want to find your niche within the country scene, then writing rock songs is a waste of time and energy.

Start general. You may not attract a large audience immediately but doing this should help you engage potential fans. "Oh, you're a country artist", they say, because they instantly recognize the style of music you're making.

Once established on a general level, you're ready to go specific. And, you can begin exploring one of many subgenres, such as bluegrass, country blues, honky tonk and beyond. You could even attempt to create your own genre.

Diversify Later

"This doesn't sound like creative freedom to me", you might say.

I will readily admit there is a difference between creating art for yourself and creating art for an audience.

Entrepreneurs understand the importance of building their audience. After all, if there's no one to sell to, there's no opportunity to be had!

"But when do I get to try something different?", you may be asking.

Look, there's nothing wrong with deviating away from your core genre here and there. Experimentation can lead to many interesting discoveries and help you stay inspired to work on your art over the long haul. So, please feel free to try different things. But for the most part, you should stick to your guns, especially early on.

There is a good time to diversify, however, and that's when you've established yourself in one genre.

If you're creative, then there's a good chance your creativity knows many expressions. But your initial goal should be to be known for one thing before you add other things to your portfolio.

It's not just creatives that struggle with this. There are plenty of entrepreneurs that suffer from shiny object syndrome too.

So, hold off on diversification until later. Establish yourself in one arena first.

Own Your Niche

It's easier to get established in a niche than it is to get established in a general market. But this isn't to suggest that it won't require hard work either way, as it likely will.

This is especially true if you're creating something in a niche that's not saturated, or mostly non-existent. If it doesn't exist, no one knows about it, which means you must create awareness for it. And, that can be challenging and costly.

That's why I said it's best to start general and then go specific. If you start with an art form people are familiar with, and then add your own flavor to it, you should have at least a small audience to draw from. And, if they like what you do, your art should spread gradually by word of mouth.

Again, we can't discount the importance of marketing, which is why I've dedicated some space to that conversation as well. So, don't wait for your fans to do all your promotion work for you.

Regardless, your goal should be to own your niche. Don't paint one neon yellow tiger and call it a day. Paint dozens or even hundreds of them. Then, begin to share these with the world. Put pictures of your paintings on your website and snag the top spot in Google. Get all your paintings to show up in Google Image Search. Be the go-to person in the neon yellow tiger space.

The Road to Profit

Understand that not everything you do will be a runaway success.

You could have done everything right and still not find an audience or make any money from your art.

So, treat this like an experiment. If necessary, go back to the drawing board and start over. Your neon yellow tigers might not strike a chord with people, but your efforts will not have been in vain. If you try your hand at something else and become known for that, your neon yellow tigers could also begin flying off the shelf.

Tools & Resources

How do I achieve creative freedom?
http://www.musicentrepreneurhq.com/creativefreedo
m

Marketing Your Art

I've talked to hundreds of business owners.

What I've discovered is that many who've freed themselves to work on high-level tasks in their businesses often engage in marketing.

That tells me a few things:

1. That marketing should be considered a high-level task.

2. That marketing is worth putting your time into.

3. That marketing can be a lot of fun.

Marketing is a skill you should master, and if you can't, you should find a marketing expert who can help you grow your business.

Either way, it's beneficial to understand the basics of marketing. Here's what you should know.

The Two Types of Marketing

In a broad sense, there are essentially two types of marketing:

1. Online marketing.

2. Offline marketing.

Both types of marketing are important.

As you can guess, online marketing refers to anything you do on the internet–blog posts, social media, emails, pay per click advertising, Search Engine Optimization (SEO) and more.

Meanwhile, offline marketing represents any marketing you conduct that isn't tied to the internet– networking, speaking engagements, print advertising, publications, trade shows and more.

It's exciting to think about everything you could be doing out there. But I think you'll find it valuable to pick your battles, especially early on.

What I mean is that novice marketers tend to spread themselves entirely too thin.

Social networks? Cool–I'm going to go register 50 accounts right now!

Don't be unrealistic. If you're just getting started, there's only one of you. You can't keep 50 separate social media accounts updated (at least not without the help of automation tools).

If I were you, I would focus on mastering one or two channels before adding more. This will help you stay focused and not take on more than you can handle.

But how do you know where you should put your time and energy? That's what I'm going to get into now.

Getting in Front of Your Audience

If you apply your creativity to your marketing, you should be able to come up with unique and disruptive ways of getting in front of your audience.

But a metal band performing at a country venue might cause a riot, so we still need to be smart and mindful about how we market ourselves if we don't want to waste our time, money and energy.

There's a social network called XING. Have you heard of it? It's essentially the LinkedIn for creatives.

You *might* be able to connect with a few people and make some fans by sharing your art on XING. I'm not going to discourage you from trying. But I can't imagine it would be the best investment of your time.

It still represents *an* opportunity. But you wouldn't prioritize it over Facebook, would you? You'd add it to your marketing mix when you had the bandwidth for it.

So, whether it's online or off, it's important to go where your audience is and have a chance of connecting with them.

The good news is that there are publications, communities, Meetup groups, forums, blogs, social networks, storefronts and eCommerce stores, and other businesses and organizations serving virtually every audience out there. There's a good chance someone has already built the audience you're trying to get in front of.

Now, you might not like the idea of competition. I understand.

But the fact that there are other people in the market you're looking to enter is usually a good sign. It means there's an opportunity to be had. Someone is making money in the niche, and you could be too.

And, as I've already pointed out, there's probably an opportunity for you to get in front of that audience.

In an online setting, that might mean guest posting on a popular industry blog. Offline, that might mean getting booked at a venue where people appreciate your style of poetry.

Ultimately, I don't care what mediums or channels you use to market your art. So long as it's driving results, and it's not violating man or God's laws, it's all fair game.

But you should still build your own platform, regardless of what other platforms you leverage. Nevertheless, it's good to be aware that you can create visibility on third-party platforms and redirect traffic to your own.

But hold the phone. If you don't know who your audience is, you wouldn't know where to begin. Don't worry–that's what the next section is about.

Identifying Your Audience

Okay, so you've made something–a poem, a play, a painting, a drawing, a song, anything–and now you want to share it with the world.

You post it to your blog and… crickets.

So, you wait a while. You're sure those comments, emails and/or purchases will come flooding in once everyone sees your brilliance.

A week later… still nothing.

Well, there are plenty of reasons why this can happen. It could be that your creation isn't as good as you thought it was. It could be that your offer isn't priced appropriately. More than likely, it's just that you don't have enough traffic coming to your blog. Fortunately, it can grow over time if you keep with it.

But to get traffic coming to your website, you first need to identify your audience and understand what they like.

I'm not suggesting that you must adjust your art to suit your audience. Sometimes this is necessary but there is an audience for practically everything out there already. Very simply, to appeal to them, you need to gain a better understanding of who they are.

One way to do this is to find artists who are already doing the kinds of things you're doing. You can then analyze the content they have on their website, look at the comments on their blog, or just examine their art for more ideas.

You could also enter their website address into a tool like Alexa or SimilarWeb and get a better sense of who their audience is. These tools will give you information on things like audience geography, top keywords the website ranks for, traffic sources, audience interests and more.

Don't forget to take advantage of Google Analytics for your website and Insights on Facebook. It's a bit technical, but there's a lot you can learn about your audience by analyzing the data these apps collect for you. Keep growing your traffic on your website and likes on Facebook, and you'll learn a lot about your audience.

Sometimes this is a fast process and sometimes it can take a long time. Either way, identifying your audience is worth the effort so stick with it!

Keep it Simple

If you can market your art effectively, you can find success as a creative entrepreneur. That's what I believe, anyway.

There's a lot that goes into marketing. So, don't be afraid to delve deeper into this world. You might end up spending a lot of time in research and study, but I promise the effort you put in won't go to waste.

Most of all, keep it simple, especially early on. The more complicated the strategy, the harder it can be to execute because it will require more of your time, effort and money. And, there's a greater chance you'll make mistakes along the way.

I would suggest creating a simple written plan to begin with. You can always adjust as necessary, especially if you find what you're doing is not working, or you know it could be improved upon.

Tools & Resources

How to Automate Your Social Media Marketing as a Musician
http://www.musicentrepreneurhq.com/automate

XING
http://www.xing.com/

Alexa
http://www.alexa.com/

SimilarWeb
http://www.similarweb.com/

Google Analytics
http://www.google.com/analytics

Building Your Platform

We are in the digital age. That being the case, it's important that we connect with people in two ways.

Today, people lead two lives—their physical life and their digital life. So, if you aren't leveraging both touch points, you're almost certainly leaving money on the table and missing opportunities.

Your Physical Life

As an artist, you have a physical presence by default.

There's a good chance you're already playing shows, attending open mics, going to art galleries, meeting people at exhibits and networking events, and so on. And, most importantly, you're making art.

You may not have a literal platform to stand on. Or, you may not have a way to get in front of new people every single day or every single week.

But at the very least, the people closest to you already know what you do. And, if they are impressed by your work, your art may already be spreading through word of mouth.

But what I've just described only represents one touch point.

Your Digital Life

If you're in the 18 to 44 age range, there's a good chance you're using social media platforms like Facebook already.

But many artists find they need to overcome their fear of sharing their work with the world.

So, let me ask you a question:

Are you currently using social media platforms to share your drawings and paintings, poetry and written works, audio and video, and so on?

If yes, good for you. If no, you may need to give some thought as to why that is.

But here's something many artists aren't clued into– *social media isn't enough.*

The Trap of Social Media

If you're reading this now, it's either because you're already a creative entrepreneur, or because you're thinking about taking a more entrepreneurial approach to your artistic career.

That being the case, relying entirely on social media is a mistake.

The problem with social media is that you don't own Facebook or Twitter or YouTube or Pinterest.

If they decide to shut down your account, there's nothing you can do about it.

And, what if these platforms go away? You lose your followers and all the momentum you've built to that point.

Smart creative entrepreneurs know this and take certain steps to connect with their audience in other ways. And, most importantly, they have a way of capturing their audience's data, namely their email addresses.

The Critical Importance of Building Your Own Platform

I love Ralph Smart, also known as Infinite Waters. His niche is spirituality, and he uploads insightful videos on the topic daily.

His primary platform is YouTube. It's the perfect place for him to share long-form content on his chosen subject matter. As of this writing, he has nearly 1.4 million subscribers.

But here's the rub. He also has a website where he shares exclusive content. His audience can also go to his website to buy his books and merchandise.

Now, there's one thing he's not doing. He's not capturing the email addresses of his followers. He may have his reasons for not doing this. But it's important to recognize that your own platform is the perfect place to do exactly that–get people to sign up for your email list.

Why am I so insistent on building your own platform and email list? *Because it reduces risk*. If a social media platform shuts you down, but you've been consistent with building your list, you won't lose your entire following.

Building Your Website & Email List

Now you know why building your own website and email list is so important.

But there are some traps you can fall into when building your website as well. There are many free or low-cost services that allow you to build a website on their platform. Some of these are well-intentioned, but again there are going to be some restrictions, and you're going to end up building on a platform that belongs to someone else.

What you should do is secure your own domain name (i.e. www.yourartistname.com) and hosting with a service like Cloudways. That way, you can back up your website at any time and save all your data. And, if you ever end up needing to switch to another hosting service, you can. This process may not be painless, but at least you won't lose your following.

As for building your email list, there are plenty of services like MailChimp that allow you to collect email addresses and communicate with your audience.

Don't sweat this point, because, again, they let you back up and store your list and even move it to another service if necessary.

Spiderweb Marketing

The importance of websites for artists is a hotly debated topic. I often hear artists say things like, "I have a Facebook Page. Do I really need a website?"

It's true that your website represents but one touch point online. There's a vast world of social media to take advantage of.

So, here's one way to think about this. Let's say there's a spiderweb and the spider is at the center. A spider, as we know, erects a web to capture his prey.

This is a good analogy for how to think about our online platforms. Your website is at the center. Your social media is the web, capturing your audience at various points. Your goal is to bring your audience back to your home, your website, to engage with you. While there, you can get them to subscribe to your email list or purchase your goods.

Everyone wins. You win because you get to communicate and sell to your audience. Your audience wins because they can interact and engage with you on a more personal level. They get the opportunity to get to know who you are and what you're about.

And, if they come to know, like and trust you, it will increase the chances of them buying from you.

Your Platform: A Foundation to Stand on

You're a creative entrepreneur. So, you should understand the importance of property. When you own a property, it's yours to do with as you please. You have complete control over it.

But you don't have complete control over social media. There's so much to see and click on. There's so much distraction. How do you ensure people see and engage with your message? The simple answer is, you don't! It's impossible to control behavior.

But on your platform, you can draw attention to what you consider most important, whether that's your music, your art, your written works, your latest video or otherwise.

Having your own platform gives you a good foundation to stand on.

Tools & Resources

Ralph Smart
http://www.ralphsmart.com/

Cloudways
http://www.musicentrepreneurhq.com/cloudways

MailChimp
http://www.mailchimp.com/

Serving Your Audience

You're at the heart of your creativity. So, you might assume that you are the most important person in your career.

I can already hear you saying, "Wait, what? I'm not?

Well, your career wouldn't be possible if not for the people that support you on your journey.

I'm talking about the people that interact with you on social media, leave comments on your blog, join your email list, buy your products and more. You can't take these people for granted.

Today, customer expectations are higher than ever. And, it's entirely too easy to leave a bad taste in people's mouths when you consistently underdeliver.

Now, I'm not saying you won't make mistakes, but your reputation is something that must be protected.

Let's talk about serving your audience as a creative entrepreneur.

Connect & Engage

Musician Jonathan Coulton was once a computer geek with a day job. Eventually, he was able to make the leap to stay-at-home dad and full-time musician.

He'd been planning to leave his job for many years to pursue music. But before long, he found himself in his mid-30s with a mortgage, a wife and a daughter. With his wife's blessing, however, he began writing and releasing one song per week.

His songs were full of novelty, with plenty of references that would make a geek smile. And, they caught on fast.

Soon, he found himself answering upwards of 100 fan emails per day. It was taking him four to five hours daily just to process all the messages.

Sound like a good problem to have? I agree. But Coulton was quick to mention that having to answer that volume of emails was a lot like working a day job.

It wasn't long before he hired an assistant to help with the overwhelming demand.

Regardless, the point should be clear–Coulton felt it important that each of his fans get a personal reply. Do you know anyone that's shown the same level of dedication to their inbox?

It's not about what you *think* you would do in a situation like that. It's about what you do when success suddenly descends on you.

Someone who's gone through the momentum of it will confirm that these are two different things.

Add Value to Your Audience

There are many ways to add value to your audience.

In the world of online marketing, marketers often employ a strategy called content marketing. Essentially, it's the act of creating content that serves and helps your target audience on an ongoing basis, ultimately ushering them onto taking a profitable action.

You need not look far to see examples of this strategy in action. For instance, have a look at SuperFastBusiness. A quick look at the blog and podcast section of the site will show content on a variety of topics online business owners would find valuable–running a membership site, how to improve your marketing funnel, engaging your community and more.

I do the same thing with The Music Entrepreneur HQ. I publish content on a variety of topics musicians and music entrepreneurs would find valuable, whether it's booking shows, designing a band logo, steps to become a professional guitar player or otherwise.

The content is free, but it serves a purpose. And that purpose is to generate traffic to the website, build trust and get visitors to subscribe to my email list or purchase a product. Content is a powerful traffic generation tool.

No matter how you go about it, giving something away for free is a great way to build your audience. You don't necessarily need to give it *all* away. But it is a good idea to think about what you can do on an ongoing basis to connect with your visitors, prospects and customers.

Understand Your Audience's Interests & Needs

It's all good and well to add value to your audience. But this won't do you much good if you don't know what they want to begin with.

Today, people vote with their attention. An often-quoted marketing stat shows that the average person's attention span is about eight seconds, which is less than a goldfish.

I don't buy into that statistic. But it is true that if you have someone's attention, they're far more likely to do business with you. People buy from those they know, like and trust. That's something that hasn't changed in a long time and it isn't about to change either.

When you are truly serving your audience, you aren't just creating content or a product. You're creating something they've specifically asked for and want.

So, you need to pay attention to your audience. Read their blog or social media comments and their emails. Survey them. Check your analytics (i.e. with Google Analytics and Facebook Insights).

There's a good chance you will build a more profitable business if you pay attention to your audience's interests and needs.

Under-Promise & Over-Deliver

When you think of "sales", what words immediately come to mind?

Pushy? Aggressive? Manipulative? Intrusive? Slimy?

I know, sometimes sales can sound like a dirty word. And most of us have that experience of being pushed into buying something we never intended to buy to begin with.

But if you're a creative entrepreneur, then the importance of sales should be obvious. Without sales, you wouldn't have revenue. That's a problem.

In business, I would suggest under-promising and overdelivering, and that flies in the face of traditional sales, which focused on getting the sale rather than serving the customer.

Before the internet, salespeople often overpromised and underdelivered, because by the time the customer had made a buying decision, the salesperson had built up her product to be the best thing since sliced bread.

That's the opposite of what you should do as a creative entrepreneur. We want to under-promise and over-deliver. That extends into anything you're selling.

We should go the extra mile to delight and surprise our prospects and customers. That will keep them coming back for more.

Be a Rock Star at Customer Service

There is a limit to what you can do as a solopreneur. So, building your team and having skilled people work in the right departments can help you manage the work involved in creating a standout customer experience.

But you know as well as I do that big companies don't always have the best customer service, right?

How many calls have you made to utility or communications companies that force you to menu surf for five to 10 minutes (i.e. "press one if you want to hear your current balance...") before you can get a real person on the other end to help you solve your problem?

Whatever you do early on to surprise and delight your customers may not be sustainable or scalable over the long haul. In other words, you may not be able to do it forever.

But it's still worth it to put your best foot forward. And, when you're ready to bring on your team, you should systematize the customer experience so that you can offer the same quality experience every single time.

Tools & Resources

Jonathan Coulton
http://www.jonathancoulton.com/

8 Tips for Getting More Superfans Through Content Marketing
http://www.musicentrepreneurhq.com/contentmarketi ng

SuperFastBusiness
http://www.superfastbusiness.com/

How to Approach Venues to Get Your Show Booked
http://www.musicentrepreneurhq.com/booked

Building Your Team

It doesn't matter whether you're a creative or an entrepreneur–a combination of both, or something in between. People in this realm often struggle with hiring.

And yet, one of the top regrets most experienced entrepreneurs have is *not hiring sooner*. So, it's clear that building a team makes a difference.

But overcoming your fears and taking that leap of faith can be scary. Simultaneously, growing your business is going to prove difficult if not impossible unless you grow with it.

So, here are some ideas on how you can overcome your objections and fears around hiring.

Why Hiring Can be a Struggle

Art is often created in isolation.

There's nothing wrong with that. But it does mean that you're probably used to working by yourself.

I believe one of the best uses of your time as a creative entrepreneur is creating. But there are a lot of things that can take away from your creative time as your business grows – bookkeeping, administrative work, sending emails, posting to social media, and a great deal more.

Many creatives just grit it and bear it. And, even when their personal bandwidth has reached its limit, they insist on doing everything themselves.

Why is that?

Many creatives feel like no one could do what they do as well as they can. I can tell you right now that this is simply not true. Not only are there people that are good at tasks you aren't, there are also people that love tasks you don't.

But if I were to boil this resistance down to a single cause, it would be fear. Creative entrepreneurs fear the costs of hiring, the training process, whether they can trust someone else to handle a specific task, and so on.

Begin Simply

Just because you need a team doesn't mean you need to create 10 new job postings today and allocate ad spend to them.

If you've never hired before, and don't have much experience working with others, it's okay to begin simply.

There are a lot of great sites out there–like Upwork and Freelancer–that allow you to post jobs and hire freelancers for one-offs or even ongoing work. Fiverr can also be helpful, but because service providers are working on the cheap (i.e. $5 plus add-ons), you won't always get the quality of work you're looking for without spending more.

I've hired freelancers often enough to know that it can be beneficial to leverage hired help in this way, especially if it allows you to focus on high level tasks.

I also have one freelancer who I've kept on over the long haul. She's my transcriptionist. Her responsibility is to create transcriptions for my podcast episodes. She is not required to do anything else. And, she always has a steady workload, because I publish new podcast episodes weekly. Even if she transcribes all my podcast episodes, I would still have other things for her to transcribe.

It's not uncommon for entrepreneurs to be feeling overwhelmed by the time they're ready to hire (because they weren't anticipating the need). And, if you're overwhelmed, you may not even have the mind space available to be thinking about who to hire, how to train them, what they need to know to do their job and so on. So, there's nothing wrong with hiring freelancers to take a load off.

Outsourcing Works Too

Laganson Graphic Design is responsible for putting together the book cover design for my last mini-book, *The Essential Guide to Music Entrepreneurship,* and they put together the cover design for this book too.

I still do quite a bit of design work myself, but if there's something specific I'm looking for, I will get Laganson to work on it for me.

Whether it's posters, infographics or book covers, there can be a lot of pressure on you as a designer when you're putting together a design for material that will be seen by a lot of people. Getting an outsider to work on your design can be helpful, because they will come up with ideas you probably wouldn't have.

Regardless of what you're trying to accomplish, you can probably find on-demand service providers, agencies or outsources that can help you. Though it's not the same as having someone in-house working for you, having a go-to person for different tasks and responsibilities can lighten your load and make your life easier. And, maybe if things work out, you can hire them part-time or full-time down the line.

Building Your A-Team

Your goal as a creative entrepreneur is to build your A-Team. If your business is growing, you don't want to be working alone or just hiring freelancers forever. You want to bring on people who can help you expand your vision full-time.

You may come across great talent as you hire and work with freelancers, outsourcers, service providers and so on. And, in some instances, you might be able to bring them on as full-time employees when you're ready.

The goal at this stage is to find people who can fit specific roles and excel in them. These people should complement your talent, experience and skills. You're not looking for people who can do what you do, unless you're trying to create a backup for yourself.

Your A-Team should be made up of people who are sharp, competent and capable. You should have buy-in from them.

When building your team, communicating your vision will prove critically important, because that's what tends to matter most to people that represent the workforce these days. They want to know what you're about and whether they resonate with it.

If you're good at what you do, eventually you will be able to make yourself redundant in your company. Now, if your endeavors involve making art, then there probably isn't any replacement for you as an artist. But you could free yourself to *just* create, wouldn't that be amazing? I know plenty of artists that want that.

Multiply Your Productivity

As a solopreneur, your productivity is going to be capped. There's going to be a limit to how much you can take on.

And, if you're always at capacity with no end in sight, you're probably going to burn out at some point. If that happens, you're not going to be able to sustain the same workload for long.

Don't get me wrong–you can still have a great business as a solopreneur, and there's nothing wrong with it. In some instances, that may even be the ideal setup.

But there is a lot involved in creating, marketing and selling art that has nothing to do with the art itself.

There's bookkeeping, managing your money, paying your bills, administrative work, data entry, answering calls and emails, and a great deal more.

Building a team can free you from having to wear so many hats and managing every aspect of your business.

And, as I've discovered, working with someone just as committed as you won't just double your productivity. Your productivity can easily triple, quadruple and even multiply well beyond that.

Tools & Resources

Upwork
http://www.upwork.com/

Freelancer
http://www.freelancer.com/

Getting Your Systems in Order

Systems? Creativity? There's *no way* these two things go together.

And yet, as I see it, to not have systems is to waste a lot of time.

Now, I will say at the outset that systems should exist to serve you–not the other way around. To serve systems, unfortunately, is to become a slave to them. And, that works about as well in business as it does in creativity.

The purpose of systems is to boost your productivity. No, scratch that–the purpose of systems is to boost your *effectiveness*.

Increase Your Effectiveness with Systems

My business coach, James Schramko holds that the obsession with productivity is generally misguided. This is because productivity is all about *getting things done*.

This is akin to using a hammer to hammer nails, drill screws and saw through two-by-fours. A hammer was intended for one of these tasks, but not all of them.

What I'm saying is this–in productivity, every task looks the same. You can't differentiate one from another. You can't help but see all of them as being equally important.

In practice, that's *never* the case. Some tasks and projects are *always* more important than others.

What matters is *effectiveness*–prioritizing things that will move the needle in your business.

I'm sure you're familiar with the 80/20 rule, which states that 80% of your results come from 20% of your efforts. If you can identify the 20% that's making a difference in your business and spend more time on that 20%, you'll be miles ahead of most.

Here's another way of looking at it:

If you're focused on urgent tasks, you're probably not dedicating enough time to important tasks. You see, low priority tasks are almost always urgent, while high priority tasks rarely are. That's an easy way to distinguish whether what you're working right now is high value.

What is a System?

Now that you understand the difference between productivity and effectiveness, it's time to define what a system is.

Systems are processes, procedures and policies. Some people know them as Standard Operating Procedures (or SOPs).

Ever since I read David Allen's *Getting Things Done: The Art of Stress-Free Productivity*, I've been using a yellow legal pad for my to-do lists, and a desktop calendar to keep track of my schedule. That is now a system embedded in my business.

Systems enable a business to scale and grow. You may be able to take your business to a certain point without systems, but inevitably there will come a point when you simply can't expand any further. To lend credence to this point, I've interviewed over 100 successful business owners and they all told me the same thing.

Systems help you identify the steps involved in every task you need to carry out, which can help you speed up your work. And, if you want to hand tasks off to your volunteers, community members or employees, you can simply give them your procedure documents and they'll be able to take over (assuming your documents are easy to understand).

The goal of this section is to introduce you to the concept of systems and not to help you earn an MBA, so for our purposes systems are *checklists*.

All Repetitive Tasks Should be Turned into Checklists

Nothing could be simpler than a checklist. It starts at step one and sequentially outlines every step necessary to complete a specific task.

Despite its simplicity, it's an elegant solution to help you improve your effectiveness.

Let me ask you a question:

Do you ever find yourself doing the same things in your business repeatedly?

I'm sure you can think of a few things, whether it's setting up your camera, answering emails, posting to social media or otherwise.

All these tasks can be–and *should* be–turned into checklists.

Why do I say that? Well, repetitive tasks may not exactly be sexy. But if you find yourself doing them all the time, there's probably a good reason for it. There's a strong chance they're important to your business. And, if you find a few that aren't, then you can take this opportunity to eliminate them.

There's nothing glamorous about posting to social media. But it needs to be done. So, you should have a checklist detailing each step that needs to be followed. Your document should contain information like when to post, what to post, what platforms to post to and so on.

Then, once you have your checklist, follow it. Not only will tasks be completed in less time (try timing yourself)–you'll also be able to achieve consistent results every time. So, with systems your overall effectiveness increases.

Harness the Power of Automation Tools

Every task you need to do should ultimately be subjected to delegation, automation or elimination.

I've covered the delegation and elimination pieces already. Now it's time to look at automation.

Does this mean that some tasks can be put on autopilot? Essentially, *yes*.

Now, I'm not necessarily talking about using AI here, although that could certainly be a part of the equation. What I'm saying is that there are plenty of apps and tools out there that can help you minimize time spent on repetitive tasks and maximize time spent on creativity.

There is almost always a setup process and sometimes a maintenance process with tools like these. But if it eases your burden and allows you to concentrate on your art, it would be worth investing into automation, would you agree?

I'll offer a couple of examples.

I've used a variety of social media scheduling tools through the years. Then, I found Meet Edgar. Meet Edgar allows you to create a library of posts and have them go out at specific times according to your calendar. Assuming you have a lot of posts queued up, your social streams will stay fresh without you constantly having to manually post to Facebook, Twitter or LinkedIn.

Similarly, I like to use a tool called Repurpose. Among other things, it will take your podcast episodes and turn them into YouTube videos automatically. Once you've connected your accounts, this all happens without your involvement. Incredible.

This is just the starting point. There are so many other great apps out there depending on what you need to automate, so don't be shy about Googling solutions that could make your life easier.

You May Not be Able to Systematize Creativity- but You Can Systematize Everything in Between

There are many aspects of creativity that can be systematized.

Consider the example of a painter. Every time they go to paint, they need to set up their easel and canvas, their paints and brushes, water jar and paper towel, and anything else they need.

Do you see how this process could be boiled down to a checklist? Even though you'll probably do this a dozen, a hundred or even thousands of times as a painter, having a checklist for your process can speed things up and help you get to the important part – painting – faster.

Tools & Resources

086 – How to Work Less & Make More as a Music Entrepreneur – with James Schramko of SuperFastBusiness
http://www.musicentrepreneurhq.com/james

Forget productivity – embrace effectiveness
http://www.musicentrepreneurhq.com/effectiveness
Getting Things Done: The Art of Stress-Free Productivity by David Allen

http://www.musicentrepreneurhq.com/gtd

Meet Edgar
http://www.meetedgar.com/

Repurpose
http://www.musicentrepreneurhq.com/repurpose

SweetProcess
http://www.sweetprocess.com/

How to Present Yourself

How you conduct yourself says a lot about who you are.

And, if people are confused about you or don't think they can trust you, you're going to end up with far fewer customers, clients, fans, followers and so on.

This isn't to suggest that you need to appeal to everyone to build a sustainable business or career. You don't need to be a people pleaser either.

But if you understand the fundamentals of how to present yourself in the best light, you will create more opportunities for yourself–not just in your creative work but also in life.

So, here are some tips on how to present yourself as a creative entrepreneur.

How to Connect with Anyone

There's simply no avoiding it–no matter what kind of work you do, you're going to be working with others –investors, partners, collaborators, vendors, suppliers and beyond.

Your people skills and ability to communicate with others will play a key role in creating meaningful connections, generating opportunities, making sales and more.

It's not necessary for you to become a pro at networking. But it would be a good idea to learn how to carry on a conversation and relate to people on a level that matters to them.

It takes time to build a rapport with others. So, your key strategy for connecting with others should be to *ask questions*. Sounds simple enough, right?

I'm going to share with you a formula I picked up in network marketing. You may think that a formula would make you stiff in conversation, but I've found it offers a lot of context and freedom once you've mastered it. The formula I refer to is called FORM, and it looks like this:

- **Family**. Where are you from? What is your background? How many siblings do you have? Do you have a spouse and kids?

- **Occupation**. What do you do for a living? Do you have any side gigs?

- **Recreation**. What do you like to do in your spare time? Where do you go to engage in your hobbies?

- **Message**. In network marketing, this is the point of the conversation where you'd "drop the message" so to speak. In other words, if you saw an opening to introduce them to your business, you would. As a creative entrepreneur, this is where you could hand them a business card, invite them to your art exhibit, share your website with them, and so on.

There you go–that wasn't so bad, was it?

Though you don't want to come across as an interrogator, in general asking questions and listening to the answers being given is a good way to connect with people.

How to Present Yourself as a Professional

There are a few things to think about when it comes to professionalism. Let's start with your clothing.

How to dress tends to be industry specific. So, men, you don't necessarily need to wear a suit all the time. And, ladies, you don't necessarily need to climb into that fancy dress for every occasion. That's a relief, right?

Do a bit of research. What do successful people in your niche wear? How do they present themselves?

Unless you're trying to be innovative or disruptive in some way, there's no need to reinvent the wheel. Go ahead, steal ideas from others.

Todd Henry is someone I've been following for quite some time. He's an author, international speaker and a well-known podcaster in the creative space. He helps creative professionals be brilliant and prolific in a sustainable way.

His attire is business casual. And, that's hardly surprising considering what he does. But it also goes to show that you don't need to be dressed to the nines to connect with your audience or fellow collaborators.

Now, it is important to be mindful of the situation. If you're going in for an important meeting, and you're going to be around a board of directors or high-level executives, then perhaps a suit or dress is in order. Just be aware of what you're getting into.

Another important factor is personal hygiene.

Again, there's no need to go over the top here. As a creative entrepreneur, there's room to experiment and express yourself. If you're planning to get your hair done up in dreads and grow a full beard, more power to you!

But at the very least, you should clean yourself daily, brush your teeth and wear deodorant or antiperspirant. Don't let small things get in the way of you making headway in your career.

In Jr. High, girls always tended to gravitate towards guys with good personal hygiene. It's such a simple thing. Unfortunately, I was one of the guys that didn't "get it" back then. Oh well.

Finally, let's talk about the basics of meeting and connecting with people.

A smile can go a long way. So, when you're greeting someone or meeting someone for the first time, smile.

When shaking hands, avoid the "limp noodle" and "death grip". Aim for the web between the thumb and index finger, and don't grab the other person's hand too early. You're not shaking their fingers or even their palm–you're shaking *their hand*.

How to be Endorsable

I don't go to church these days. But I spent a good part of my life attending.

One of the most powerful lessons I learned in a sermon was this idea of being "endorsable".

When people are thinking about whether to work with you, they're going to do their due diligence on you.

They're going to read up on you online, determine what others have had to say about you, observe your general behavior and so on.

Now, inevitably, these people are going to end up with a mixed opinion of who you are. Not everyone is going to speak positively of you, as I'm sure not everyone speaks positively of me.

But this can work to your advantage. As it turns out, when buying a product on Amazon, people generally like to see both positive and negative reviews. And, unless the reviews are on the far side of negative, it won't stop them from buying.

So, it's important to understand that you are the cumulative effect of your attitudes, actions and behaviors. It's okay to have a few strikes against you. You're human.

But the greatest opportunities in your career will come from being endorsable.

Here are a few qualities I've identified as being important when it comes to being endorsable:

- **Be accountable**. Show up early and stay late. Be accountable to yourself and to others. Keep your meetings and finish your to-do lists.

- **Be dependable**. Complete your work on time. Be prepared for meetings, exhibits, speaking engagements or presentations, performances and so on.

- **Maintain a great attitude**. People love working with those who demonstrate enthusiasm for their work. You will encounter hardships while building your business or career, so don't let that get you down. Stoke the flames of your passion by committing to your personal growth.

- **Be trustworthy**. Keep sensitive matters private. Secure other people's information (i.e. their contact information).

- **Be willing to work hard**. Work at your craft even when no one's looking. Don't be afraid to make sacrifices when you need to whether it's turning off the TV, getting up early or staying up late.

You Are What You Do

What you say doesn't matter as much as what you do.

I can more readily tell what someone values by watching their actions rather than what they say.

So, don't make promises you can't keep. In business, you should always make it your goal to under-promise and overdeliver.

You are defined by what you do, not by what you say. Remember that.

Tools & Resources

Todd Henry
http://www.toddhenry.com/

How Can You Become More Endorsable as a Musician or Music Entrepreneur?
http://www.musicentrepreneurhq.com/endorsable

How to Think

This is what life and business strategist Tony Robbins had to say about success:

80% of success is psychological.

So, your success is less contingent on *what you do*, which only accounts for 20% of the results you achieve, and is more contingent on *how you think*, which accounts for 80% of the results you get.

Regardless of whether you buy into this notion, I think you'll agree that your mindset will play a critical role in your longevity and ultimate success as a creative entrepreneur.

Embrace Your Inner Entrepreneur

There's a difference between how an employee thinks and how an entrepreneur thinks.

An employee works for money and other people.

An entrepreneur has money and other people work for them.

This statement changed my life.

As you're first getting started in business, you will likely be doing everything yourself. And, it is a good idea to get a feel for every task that needs to be handled in your business. Being a generalist rather than a specialist can be an asset as a business owner.

But as you begin to grow your business, you're going to want to eliminate, delegate or automate tasks that you aren't good at or don't enjoy. Your goal should be to work in your strength zone as much as possible and to move away from tasks that aren't the best use of your time or energy.

Don't be afraid to seek help. I know it can be hard, especially if you're a perfectionist, but the reality is that you can't do it all by yourself. You will require the help of others to build towards your goals and dreams.

The number one regret many entrepreneurs have is *not hiring sooner*. So, hire early and begin paying others for repetitive and mundane tasks that take away from you engaging in high-level activity.

Develop a Long-Term View of Your Career or Business

An entrepreneur always thinks long-term because they know that short-term thinking can get them into trouble.

An entrepreneur understands that it may take two, five or even 10 years to achieve their desired level of success. They understand that they will encounter challenges and obstacles on their journey. They recognize that they may need to acquire new knowledge, develop new skills and seek out the mentorship of others as they grow their business.

When we allow ourselves to think short-term, generally we make pleasure-based decisions. We seek out instant gratification and look for ways to *feel good now*.

This may help you generate *some* happiness in the immediate. But it will be fleeting.

Entrepreneurs make decisions that they know will make them happier long-term. They delay gratification. They make sacrifices now based on the overarching vision of what they know their life can be.

I'm not suggesting that you shouldn't enjoy the journey. If the journey itself isn't pleasurable to you, then you might be on the wrong path! You're probably seeing your business as means to an end rather than a value-generating machine.

Business isn't just about the money you make and the freedom you create for yourself. It's also about the people you impact and the difference you make in the world. It's about the challenges you overcome, the transformation you go through as an individual and the fulfillment you derive from it.

Today, there are many entrepreneurs that make short-sighted decisions about their health and well-being. They wear long hours at the office like a badge of honor. Even if they aren't paying a price for it now, they will later, whether it's in the form of health challenges, relationship challenges or otherwise.

So, it's important to identify the extremes of short-sightedness. Some people are fundamentalists. Some are slackers. Both extremes are undesirable. Let's learn to be aggressive and sustainable at the same time.

Be Consistent & Persistent in Applying Yourself to Your Work

As a creative entrepreneur, you should understand the value of consistency.

Each year, many people set out to exercise and lose weight, write a book, learn a new skill or hobby and so on. But when push comes to shove, they don't follow through on their goals.

Why is that?

First, developing a habit takes time. As we move towards our goals, we should be looking to adopt habits that continually move us in the direction of our chosen destination.

Second, many people fail at consistency. They might hit the gym a few times as the New Year begins, but then they stop going. Here's what happened–they didn't develop the habit of going to the gym, so it never became a part of their routine.

But what does it mean to be consistent?

First, I'll tell you what consistency is *not*:

It's not spending 15 minutes on Monday, three hours on Tuesday, seven minutes on Wednesday, one hour on Thursday and 20 minutes on Friday.

In that example, your average was roughly 56 minutes, right? *Wrong*.

Your average was seven minutes. If you had spent *at least* 56 minutes at the task every single day, then your average would have been 56 minutes. But you didn't. On Wednesday, you only engaged for seven minutes. So, that's what your average would be.

As you can imagine, a higher average is more desirable, regardless of what tasks you're engaging in.

So, determine what's important to you. Then, start creating a routine around the key areas you've identified. Schedule in the activities you need to engage in every single week. Finally, follow through on the promises you've made to yourself.

Become an Expert Problem-Solver

Entrepreneurship is like skydiving without a parachute and problem solving on the way down.

Does that sound scary? It sure can be.

So, it's important to be able to look at problems from a variety of angles and seek out solutions beyond the obvious.

In my experience, it's hard to find expert problem-solvers. So, it's no wonder that so many people fail in business.

Fundamentally, the job of an entrepreneur is to solve problems.

Many people think success occurs when everything is working perfectly in their lives. But the opposite is often true—success is messy. You could even say that the more successful you are, the more fires you'll have to put out.

Get good at thinking outside the box and coming up with many ways of handling a problem. And, don't just think about the things you're willing to do—also consider the things you're *not* willing to do.

I'm not talking about violating the laws of man or God. I'm talking about the things that make you uneasy, such as selling your car or home, taking out a second mortgage or other short-term lifestyle sacrifices that could help you live an amazing life in the long-term.

Entrepreneurs do what nobody's willing to do now so they can live like nobody can later.

Develop a Rock-Solid Mindset

This is what it all comes down to. The exact details of how you think don't matter as much as your attitude. When your attitude is right, the facts don't count.

So, work on your mindset. If you don't, the slightest of problems might stop you dead in your tracks. But if you do strengthen your mindset, you'll blow right by many obstacles that will present themselves on your journey.

Tools & Resources

Tony Robbins explains why 80 percent of success is
psychological
http://www.musicentrepreneurhq.com/psychological

How to create more options for yourself
http://www.musicentrepreneurhq.com/options

Problem-Solving: An Essential Skill for Music
Entrepreneurs
http://www.musicentrepreneurhq.com/problem

Developing Yourself

Maybe you don't believe in all that "personal development crap".

I get where you're coming from. I think it's relatively normal to be a skeptical, especially as a creative.

And, through the ages, creatives have a history of being exploited. No wonder we're always on guard.

But if I decided not to share about personal development with you, I believe I would be doing you a major disservice.

That's because personal development has helped me in more ways than I can count. It's gotten me to the point where my mind is quieter than it's ever been and I'm able to act on what I say is important to me.

Isn't there something in your life you say you want to do, but you keep putting off? What's going on there?

It's not that you don't know *what* to do. You probably know the *exact* steps you need to take. And yet, you're stopped by something.

You don't need to be told how to lose weight. You already know that you need to eat less and exercise more. Has that knowledge changed anything in your reality?

This is where personal development comes in. It has the potential to change all that.

Get the Reading Habit

Some of the most popular posts on The Music Entrepreneur HQ website have to do with books.

The stats show that people don't do a whole lot of reading once they leave college or university. But maybe creatives are the exception. I personally know at least a few creatives who actively read to stimulate their mind and generate new ideas.

So, maybe you don't need to be told to read. Where you may be thwarted is in *what* to read.

Now, any kind of reading is beneficial. It keeps your mind sharp. It makes you a better writer. And, it can help you generate new ideas.

But if fiction books are all you read, you should consider expanding your horizons a bit. I want to challenge you to dig into topics like:

- Personal development and self-help.

- Leadership and management.

- Business and entrepreneurship.

- Marketing and promotion.

- Finances and money management.

- Spirituality and beliefs.

This is where growth happens. It's okay if most of your reading is dominated by fiction. But consider adding a little bit of personal development material into the mix.

Listening is a Two-Way Street

Another great resource for personal development is audio. Podcasts, audio courses and audiobooks are the obvious place to look.

You can subscribe to podcasts entirely for free, and there's plenty of great content out there, regardless of what topic you're interested in learning about.

You could even listen to industry or competitor podcasts to get a sense of what's going on in your niche and what your peers are up to.

Audio courses can usually be found through independent providers–typically entrepreneurs or educators, much like yourself, who are creating educational content to help people in their niche. Cost will vary, but most of this material is quite helpful. Udemy is a great source for courses on a variety of topics.

As for audiobooks, I recommend using a site like Audible, which is an Amazon-owned company that sells audiobooks. I think it's best to read *and* listen to books, not just one or the other. But whether you want to buy audiobook versions of the books you already have or pick up books you don't own is up to you.

Go Old-Fashioned

There used to be a time when people would apprentice under a master to learn their craft. Students had mentors they could turn to when they didn't understand something or needed guidance.

As an entrepreneur, you should have a mentor (or even a group of mentors) you can depend on. Don't try to do it all alone. Don't get stuck in your own head.

I've made many poor decisions because I didn't have a 360-degree view of what was happening in my business. If I had asked a few of my friends and mentors for their opinions, I probably could have avoided some of those mistakes.

When you're working hard, you can easily lose sight of what matters. This is especially true if you're on the verge of burning out, or you're already burnt out.

So, don't rely on your own brain for everything. It got you to where you are, but it may not be able to get you to where you want to go. Get guidance and feedback from other brains on an ongoing basis.

Since mentors can see things you can't, they can also help cause breakthrough in your business or career.

Seek out mentorship. Find someone who's accomplished things you'd like to accomplish and ask for their advice.

And, if you absolutely can't find or connect with anyone who's willing to mentor you, consider who you'd like to be mentored by, and read their books or listen to their podcast.

It's All About How You Enter a Room

Please go to events and conferences, and don't get too caught up in what's good or bad. You'll figure that out as you go.

Learning is all well and good. But if you don't get into groups to learn from others, be present with them, and discuss and act on what you've been learning, it doesn't do you much good. I'll talk about why that is a little later.

Some of my biggest breakthroughs have come as result of going to seminars. Sure, there are some books and podcasts that have had a huge impact on me too. But of the hundreds of books I've read, there are only been a dozen or so that made a difference. Of the thousands of podcasts, I've listened to, I'd venture to guess it's only a few dozen that made a real difference for me.

Now, I'm not going to give up on books or podcasts. But it's altogether too easy to hole up in your ivory tower and read books and listen to audio and think you're making progress. Plus, it's comfortable.

Conferences and events, on the other hand, can shed light on what people have done with the material you're learning, and how they got it out of their head into a form that lives in the real world. And, that's the only place it truly lives.

Get into the Game

What you learn makes no difference unless it exists in the world.

And, I'm sorry to be the one to break the news, but nothing that lives in your head lives in the world. Whatever is in your head is not real.

This is the reason I encourage people to *write* their goals down with pen and paper. Once you've done this, your goals exist in a material sense. But they did not exist prior to you writing them down.

So, act on what you learn. Test it out for yourself. Learning makes no difference unless it takes physical form.

Clear the Way for Something New

I used to think that personal development was all about more, better or different.

But what I've discovered is that there is no breakthrough in more, better or different. You can improve a little bit every single day. But that doesn't lead to quantum leaps in your personal growth or mindset. Doing more of something, doing it better or doing it differently is what you've been doing your whole life–and you may have seen some change. But I'm guessing you haven't seen much breakthrough.

I now believe that personal development is about clearing the space for what you want in your life. If you can't seem to get started on something you know is important to you, it's because there's mental, emotional and/or physical clutter you need to unload. It's because you need to cause completion in areas where you feel blocked and incomplete.

Once you've made the space for it, creating new possibilities becomes easy.

Tools & Resources

009 – The Value of Personal Development in Building a Music Career
http://www.musicentrepreneurhq.com/development

011 – The Importance of Reading Books in Personal Development
http://www.musicentrepreneurhq.com/reading

014 – The Importance of Listening to Audio in Personal Development
http://www.musicentrepreneurhq.com/listening

010 – Do You Have Mentorship in Your Life?
http://www.musicentrepreneurhq.com/mentorship

6 Value-Adding Podcasts I Enjoy Listening To (on Music, Business, Creativity & Social Media)
http://www.musicentrepreneurhq.com/podcasts

008 – Get in the game – don't just sit on the sidelines
http://www.musicentrepreneurhq.com/game

Udemy
http://www.udemy.com/

Audible
http://www.audible.com/

Managing Your Money

Money is a charged topic for most.

But your ability to create a sustainable and lasting career or business hinges on your financial smarts. So, it needs to be addressed, regardless of how uncomfortable or emotional it makes us feel to talk about it.

Managing your money well could mean the difference between releasing a new album every single year and not.

And, if you're not a musician, just substitute the term "album" for book, painting, play or whatever applies.

Here are some tips on how to manage your money.

Forget What You Think You Know About Money

If you're happy with your financial life, then disregard this section and move on. But if things aren't going well for you, keep reading.

First, I want you to forget everything you know about money. And, if you're honest with yourself, you'll recognize that this pool of knowledge is very small anyway.

You may know a thing or two about mortgages, mutual funds, TFSAs (Canada) or Roth IRAs (U.S.).

But the banks don't have your best interests at heart, and that's likely where your financial "smarts" come from.

Banks never taught me anything about managing my money. They only tried to push more products on me.

"You don't have a mortgage? Oh my god!" they would say. "You should get one. You could totally buy a house."

I once had a mortgage. I'm not a big believer in them anymore. I also had mutual funds and TFSAs. Granted, I think a TFSA is perhaps the most benevolent product available, and beneficial if used correctly.

Regardless, if you went to "bank university" like most people did, and you're confused about your money, you're probably like most others out there. You can't learn how to master your money from an entity that's there to sell you financial services, even though some are worthwhile.

Have you emptied your mind of what you think you know? Good—then we're ready to talk about real financial smarts.

Pay Yourself First

If we want to succeed in our financial lives, first we must trade in what we think we know for time-tested and proven strategies.

Here's one strategy worth implementing immediately—*pay yourself first*.

This is where a lot of people get it wrong because they assume someone else will take care of them later in life, whether it's the government, the company they work for, their family or their friends.

The problem with this is that government is actively reducing and eliminating pension programs, and I can almost guarantee that the company you work for is not interested in keeping you on payroll longer than they must.

Your family and friends are either going through or will be going through the same financial troubles you are and won't have any more money to deal with the inevitable than you do.

Utility companies aren't going to come to your rescue either. No to be morbid, but they will happily stick your other family members with pending bills when you pass away.

And, last but certainly not least, credit card companies could care less what financial state you're in. They will keep stacking on the fees to get as much money as they possibly can out of you over the long haul.

So, the only person that cares about your financial future is you. Regardless of whether you believe this, it should give you pause.

So, when money comes in, you should pay at least 10% of that money into savings right away. It doesn't matter if you can't pay your utility bills in full. It doesn't matter if you're going to be late on that credit card payment. Pay yourself first.

I'm not telling you to go and ruin your credit. All I'm saying is that after you've paid yourself, you can problem-solve the rest later. You're a creative entrepreneur. You're resourceful. There's always a way.

I would sooner bet on my own future than willingly hand over all my money to some faceless corporation that could care less about my financial wellbeing.

Create 3 Categories of Savings

This is something I picked up from Tony Robbins and Ramit Sethi and it has worked well for me. It's not a flawless system by any means, but it's a good way to think about savings.

Many people only have one savings account into which they pay into. And, you're a step ahead of most if that happens automatically or on a planned schedule.

But I've found it helpful to create three categories of savings. They are:

1. **Emergency fund**. You should save six to nine months' worth of expenses into this account. That way, if anything comes up (and it always does), you'll have money to cover it.

2. **Dream fund**. Everyone has trips they want to take, things they want to buy, occasions they want to celebrate. Don't put this off indefinitely. Begin putting money into your dream fund right away so you can go and experience and enjoy life.

3. **Aggressive growth fund**. Once your
    emergency and dream funds have been
    furnished, you're ready to build your
    aggressive growth fund, which will be used to
    invest. This is money *you wouldn't mind
    losing*. When investing, it's always better to
    be playing with money you could live without.
    In an ideal world, you wouldn't lose it, but
    that possibility always exists in investing.

As for what to invest in, I believe lifecycle funds are
the best bet for most people. If you want to be more
hands on, then index funds might be more to your
liking.

Reinvest in Yourself & Your Future

Money is a tool.

As creative entrepreneurs, it is imperative that we
learn how to use this tool to further our art, careers,
and businesses.

What do most people do after they've just earned,
won, or been given a lot of money? Waste it!

As a business owner, you should understand the value
of reinvesting in yourself. If you have extra money,
put it back into your business.

The reason you made all that money probably had
something to do with your creativity and art to begin
with. So, if you prioritize reinvesting in yourself and
your future, you can keep growing your business, thus
setting yourself up to earn more down the line.

Your business needs to be fed and nurtured. So, keep feeding it and keep nurturing it as you're able.

Be Proactive About Your Money

Many of us tend to believe that if we just had more money, all our problems would go away.

What we don't realize is that if we just became better managers of the money we have, we'd be able to solve many of these problems without additional resources.

This isn't to suggest that it won't be hard work. But instead of counting on a windfall, learn to count your pennies and understand where they're being spent. Learn to allocate your funds to things and people you care about. If you keep at this, you will make headway in your financial life.

Engaging in Creative Alchemy

In 2017, I defined Creative Alchemy as follows:

> *Creative alchemy is the art of combining your skills and talents to create something unique.*

Now, just so you know, this idea is entirely separate from the book of the same title, by Marlo Johnson.

I know plenty of creatives that aren't just good at one thing. Some who play music also paint. Some designers are also sculptors. And, still others engage in just about every artistic discipline imaginable.

Entrepreneurs can't help but connect the dots between seemingly desperate entities and see the possibilities.

If you're a musician that also likes to paint, then there's almost certainly a way of bringing the two mediums together.

For instance, you could host a CD release party/art exhibition hybrid event. Or, your paintings could become your album artwork.

We see creative alchemy in the niche business world as well. Consider the example of Nerd Fitness, which is a nerd-friendly fitness website with gamification elements that make the process of getting in shape more fun. So, it's a hybrid community for nerds who also want to feel and look their best.

If you don't consider yourself multitalented, or you'd prefer to dedicate yourself to a single artform, that's fine. Creative Alchemy may not be for you. But if you're beginning to see some possibilities emerging, read on.

Do Everything You Love

Emilie Wapnik is the founder and creative director of Puttlylike. Her website is a community dedicated to a group of people she calls "multipotentialites".

As I've already shared, there are creative and artistic people who are good at a lot of different things. Wapnik is one of those individuals and she encourages her tribe to pursue every passion they have, without compromise.

Now, let's be realistic here–you need to go about this in a structured way. If you don't, you're not going to get anything done.

This might mean choosing what project to focus on right now, maybe for a 30- to 90-day timeframe, while you forsake all other interests. Or, maybe you could triage projects and work on the top two or three that you find most compelling. And, as you finish one, you could bring another in.

If you visit Wapnik's website and read a few of her blog posts, you'll certainly get some ideas on how to develop that type of structure around your projects.

I don't think Creative Alchemy is a license to pursue everything you want to do simultaneously. It's the discipline to take massive action on what you want to do now so that you can free up your time to engage in the next thing you want to do later, and then the next.

But if Creative Alchemy is something that has captured your imagination, then recognize that there is a way to try your hand at every artistic medium that intrigues you.

And, ultimately, it's the practice of combining these passions in meaningful ways. But to do this right, you will need to be a both/and thinker rather than an either/or thinker.

Live Like There's No Tomorrow

Another Creative Alchemist I've had the pleasure of talking with is Jules Schroeder, Founder & Visionary of Unconventional Life. She was a guest on my podcast, and I was a guest on hers.

If you visit her personal website, you will quickly see that her interests and passions range from music and public speaking to travel and Acro dance, and a great deal more. And, her visitors have even told her that her website is a little all over the place.

But Jules' story is positively inspiring. In 2015, she got into a wakeboarding accident that left her paralyzed in her neck. Apparently, she was visited by a white figure and six black shadow council members in her hospital bed. She was then told that she had more work to do in the world and was asked whether she wanted to continue.

Unwilling to go on paralyzed, her neck miraculously forged together, and she got a second lease on life.

So, she made a vow to make the most of her time here. No wonder she's so motivated and action-oriented, right?

I like the idea of "living like there's no tomorrow", because in a very real sense, today is all there is. Yesterday is a memory. Tomorrow will just be another today. So, it's all about what you make of the now. And, now is now.

If you had no constraints in your life–temporal, financial, physical, mental, emotional, psychological or otherwise–what would you do? What would you pursue? What would your life look like?

People let a variety of things stop them from experiencing and engaging in life, and it ranges from a "sore leg" all the way to a debilitating health condition. You can't move ahead by "coping" with this. You can only move ahead by clearing this clutter and making space for the new.

I'm not making light of any disadvantages, any challenges, any problems or issues you may have. But just know that many have let those things stop them from pursuing their dreams. Will you?

Connect the Dots

This book is not about me. It's about you.

I was somewhat reluctant in profiling myself in this section of the book. But as a purveyor of Creative Alchemy, I felt it was my responsibility to share.

I don't have a shortage of ideas when it comes to combining my skills and talents in compelling and unique ways.

As my bio says, I'm a musician, studio engineer, author and content creator, designer, teacher, speaker, coach, entrepreneur, investor and community builder. And that's the short list!

I'll give you one example of where many of my talents could all come together: video.

For instance, I could utilize my art, my graphics, my music and my voice to create unique video content. It would be a lot of work, because it's the meeting place of several disciplines. But if I brought it all together, I know I could create something compelling.

In my experience, combining passions in this way isn't something you would ever be able do inside of a job. That's partly what makes it so counterintuitive.

But there are many aspects to creative entrepreneurship that are counterintuitive. So, don't fight against it. Embrace the tension. That's where the growth happens.

You Aren't Limited to Just One Thing

I will never discount the importance of focus.

But just because you're focused on one thing doesn't mean you can't be focused on many things.

Meanwhile, focusing on many things *at once* is a challenge. And, you would need to manage your schedule extraordinarily well to do it all at once. Even then, you're going to risk burnout.

But as a mentor of mine once explained, we can all handle about two or three things simultaneously. So, don't overload yourself. Decide what matters most to you and pursue that. Choose two or three things and take massive action on those.

And, when it comes to Creative Alchemy, you're allowed to combine several mediums. Yes, it will be more work. You will need to allow for more time to complete each project you work on. But you can also captivate the world by fusing different disciplines together. That's what's cool about it.

Tools & Resources

Nerd Fitness
http://www.nerdfitness.com/

045 – The Rise of Creative Alchemy
http://www.musicentrepreneurhq.com/alchemy

046 – The Rise of Creative Alchemy Part 2
http://www.musicentrepreneurhq.com/alchemy2

Puttylike
http://www.musicentrepreneurhq.com/puttylike

Unconventional Life
http://www.unconventionallifeshow.com/

Jules Schroeder
http://www.julesschroeder.com/

108 – Finding Your Purpose & Living Your Passion – with Jules Schroeder of Unconventional Life
http://www.musicentrepreneurhq.com/jules

Multitalented? How to Fuse Your Business and Artistic Passion into Your Life
http://www.unconventionallifeshow.com/multitalented-how-to-fuse-your-business-and-artistic-passion-into-your-life/

Conclusion

As important as strategy and tactics are, there's one thing I would consider more important than that–namely, *mindset*.

In case you hadn't noticed, I haven't filled in all the blanks for you. Ultimately, it's up to you to figure out how all the puzzle pieces of creative entrepreneurship fit together.

Why do I say that? Because tactics change all the time. Though I've referred to some tactics in this guide, it was more to give you examples of what could be done than to hand you a rulebook.

I don't think it would be an exaggeration to say that there are as many ways to approach your marketing as there are to approach your art. And, there are many ways to approach business too.

You could even reverse engineer and copy what someone else has done and not achieve the same results. Why does that happen?

For one, you may not have access to all the information you need. It's possible you missed a key ingredient that made it all work for someone else. There might be a few things they're keeping quiet about too.

But I think it's also fair to say that what works for one may not work for another. Additionally, it's possible that in the time it took for your mentors and heroes to become successful, there were significant shifts in technology or the market you didn't even notice.

If you're old enough to recall, a little over 10 years ago, the internet's most popular social network, MySpace, was quickly overtaken by a little company called Facebook.

Not that MySpace hasn't recovered some of its former glory since then, but now it serves a niche audience as opposed to the social networking masses.

So, if you were still using MySpace to market your art in 2008, you were quickly falling behind the times. Facebook was the place to be.

Do you see what I mean when I say that tactics change drastically from one day to the next? Honestly, even if you were studying the market and watching the data every single day, there are some things you simply wouldn't be able to pick up or predict. Technology is a disruptive force in the world of business.

Amid all these changes, there's one thing that doesn't change, and that's the need for a strong mindset. If you can get this right, a lot of other things will tend to fall into place.

Whether you like it or not, if you're doing something worthwhile, there will be those who oppose, criticize, ostracize and reject you.

So, how you handle that makes all the difference.

Will you quit when the going gets rough? Or will you keep going?

It's easy to become precious about your art. After all, it's your creation. You gave birth to it. It doesn't feel good to have your art rejected by someone who doesn't even understand what you went through to create it.

Unfortunately, it happens. I even know a musician who received death threats because of how hated he was.

And, I don't think there's any getting around it– mistakes will be made. I've certainly made my share of mistakes in creativity and business, and I'm learning all the time. And, the good news is I have yet to make a mistake I haven't been able to recover from.

I like to look at every potentially negative experience as an opportunity to learn something.

The reason I've added the word "potential" here is because even seemingly negative experiences can be important turning points in your business–the moment a lightbulb comes on and everything changes.

At times, negative experiences are springboards onto more positive experiences.

It's rarely if ever easy when you're going through it in the moment. But if you take some time to reflect and think about what went wrong, you can course correct and come back stronger than before.

Thinking and reflecting is something most people don't do enough of. But as a creative entrepreneur, surely you see how valuable it can be.

So, how can we get our thinking right? What does it mean to build a strong mindset?

Unfortunately, there is no quick fix that I'm aware of. But over time, we're all capable of growing and becoming more than we are right now. Like working out, we can build our mindset muscle if we're steady and consistent.

And, most of what you need to know is in a couple of earlier chapters on **How to Think** and **Developing Yourself**. Revisit these again and again until it all sinks in.

If there's anything to add, it would be this–be consistent. Don't give up on your personal growth. Keep going.

You might read a few boring books or listen to a few podcasts that are talking about things you already know. But don't let that stop you. Don't write it all off as pointless.

The best investment you can make is the investment in yourself.

Now, I'm not saying you should worry about something that hasn't even presented itself in your reality. Far from it.

But as my mentors once taught me, it's best to dig your well before you're thirsty. That means to prepare for the road ahead.

As human beings, when problems come up, we look for ways to solve them. Sometimes we handle them well. Sometimes we don't. But we cross those bridges as we come to them, not *before*.

To become anxious about something that doesn't exist in your reality now is to give your power over to something that isn't even real.

As a creative entrepreneur, it's your job to become an expert problem solver. You need to train yourself to see beyond the obvious. Most of the time, there isn't just one way to solve a problem. There are many ways. So, get good at identifying the many paths that exist to the destination you're trying to reach.

Last but certainly not least, *please enjoy the journey*. Celebrate your wins, even if they are small. Connect with others you can share your journey with. Do something that fulfills you, as life is simply too short to spend a lot of time doing something you don't even enjoy.

Acknowledgements

First, I'd like to thank Frederick Tamagi for coming up with the idea for this book. You are my biggest supporter.

Second, I want to thank my many mentors and coaches, even those who may have only helped from a distance. Unfortunately, I'm sure to forget someone, but here's the short list–James Schramko, Ezra Firestone, Fizzle, Todd Henry, Tony Robbins, Ramit Sethi, Jack Conte, Bob Baker, Pat Flynn, Robert Kiyosaki, David Allen, Neil Patel, Eric Siu and Pastor Anthony Greco. This book would not be possible if not for the many things I've learned from you.

Third, I'd like to thank The Indie YYC inner community–Wakefield Brewster, Lisa Murphy-Lamb, Jonathan Ferguson, Stacey Walyuchow, Karlo Keet, Stefano Valdo–and anyone else who ends up joining our wonderful creative community. Likewise, I'd like to thank anyone and everyone who's chosen to participate in our events.

Finally, I'd like to thank *you,* the reader, whoever you may be–fan, follower, friend, family member, sibling, parent or even stranger. This would not be possible without you.

Let's Stay in Touch

If you'd like to find out more about what I've shared with you in this book, head on over to MusicEntrepreneurHQ.com. From blog posts to podcasts to videos, there's so much for you to learn and discover that will help you on your journey as a creative entrepreneur.

If you have any questions or comments regarding this book, feel free to email me at david@dawcast.com. I'd love to hear from you.

I look forward to connecting with you on social media as well:

Facebook: facebook.com/davidandrewwiebe

Twitter: @davidawiebe

Instagram: @davidandrewwiebe

Medium: @davidawiebe

May this book bless you on your creative journey.

Also by David Andrew Wiebe

The New Music Industry: Adapting, Growing, and
Thriving in The Information Age
http://www.musicentrepreneurhq.com/ebook

How to Record, Promote & Sell Your New Music
Release – Single, EP or Album
(co-authored with Goemon5)
http://www.musicentrepreneurhq.com/album

The Essential Guide to Music Entrepreneurship:
2018 Edition
http://www.musicentrepreneurhq.com/essential

The Music of David Andrew Wiebe

Shipwrecked... My Sentiments (2006)
http://www.davidandrewwiebe.com/shipwrecked

Fragments (2016)
http://www.davidandrewwiebe.com/fragments

Don't Wait Too Long (2016)
http://www.davidandrewwiebe.com/wait

Hope (2016)
http://www.davidandrewwiebe.com/hope

Waves (2017)
http://www.davidandrewwiebe.com/waves

Your Eyes Give It Away (2017)
http://www.davidandrewwiebe.com/eyes

Christmas Surf (2017)
http://www.davidandrewwiebe.com/surf

Fire Your God (2018)
http://www.davidandrewwiebe.com/fire